AF708808

Labyrinths of the Delta

Acknowledgments

Some of these poems have appeared in *New Letters*, *Greenfield Review*, *Europe*, *Syracuse Review*, *The Madison Review*, *Praxis*, *The Pale Fire Review*, *Prism*, and *For Neruda/Chile*.

ISBN 0-912678-67-4

Cover photograph: Equatorial Forest, Urhobo, Niger-Congo, Rattle, wood, shells, 14 1/8 x 5 x 6 (35.9 x 12.7 x 15.2), The University of Iowa Museum of Art, Iowa City, Iowa, The Stanley Collection.

The Greenfield Review Press
R.D. 1, Box 80
Greenfield Center, NY 12833

There is no night so long that it will not give way to the light of day.

—Ngugi wa Thiongo, *Petals of Blood.*

CONTENTS

Part I: The Sentence

Jewels 1
When Your God Is a Pander 2
My Share 3
The New Warriors 4
My Heart 5
Latitudes 6
The Student Takes His Leave 7
The Sentence 9
The Mask 11
Wanted: Disrespect 12
When We Have to Fly 13
Exile 14
Granny's Blessing 15
I Will Be a Bluejay 16
Movement 17
A Bottle in the Pit 18
After the Flight 21
When I Am Alone 22
Labyrinths of the Delta 23
The Hunters 28
We Know 30
Chicho 31
Africa Now 32
Indirect Song 33
Conscripted Sweat 34
Antithesis 35
Message of Lust 36
To the Bull 38
Death of the Warrior 39
Revealing the Secret 41
At the United Nations Gallery 42
To a Black Student 43
I Flew with the Kite 44
Into Your Hands 45
The Nail on the Wall 46
Behind Us 47

My Daughter's Knowledge 48
For My Child in Hospital 49
Fidelity 51
Best Wishes 52
Working 54
Visit to American Indians 55
Montreal 56
Strategies of Borno 57
A Verdict of Stone 58

Part II: The Struggle to Be Free

Give Me Light 61
Words 62
Calls 63
Debate on Nation-Building 64
Mosquitoes 66
Harsh Words 68
My Face 69
Exchanging Songs 70
We Are Many 72
The Cross 73
Ughelli 74
Waiting 75
Mirrors 78
I Sing of Love 79
We Are Not Alone 80
On Receiving a Rejected Manuscript 81
I Am Going to Be Rich 82
Alms from Severe Gods 83
And . . . 84
Song 86
Perils 87
Vigil 88
The Solace 89
Beauties 90
Blood Bank 91
In the Struggle to Be Free 92
On the Road 93
Mounting Desires 94

Theme Song 95
The Problem of Filling and Refilling 96
It Sounds More Clearly 97
Upon the Plateau 98
Anything Is Possible 99
Recoiling 100
The Bitter Smile 102
Beneath the Skin 103

Part I: The Sentence

For Anne, my wife.

For all these wan roads
I am pushed to follow, are my
own conceit. A simple muttering
elegance, slipped in my head
pressed on my soul, is my heart's
worth.

—Amiri Baraka.

JEWELS

The view from here is a rainbow:
Boa-constrictors and diamonds. I have to slay
The serpents to wear celestial jewels —

My fears are animals masked with humanity;
They stalk me into the recesses of the mind,
Throw me down, and hurt my born-again resolve.

To arrive here, I crossed a wilderness
Trailing a pilgrim who steeled his faith
despite the cubs that roamed his heart.

I have now abandoned the home in which
I coupled with a succubus;
I no longer need a talisman to get back to my senses.

My army is gathered for a thrust;
An earthy landscape separates me from victory.
The jewels beckon me with a flash.

WHEN YOUR GOD IS A PANDER

A king whose desires threaten to disrobe him
Invokes the mystique of his crown, an eagle in the forest.
Possessed by his feather-decked god, he fills his hands
With a thousand schemes, some really mean things.

He seeks dominion over frontiers, an absentee lord;
He seeks partnership in the moonlit room of songs.
He seeks sovereignty over deserted islands,
And daringly plants his flag in a disputed wilderness.

What woman hears the god's favourite and will not abandon
Her chores? His voice moves the street to the arena,
And there the eternal suitor — who outsings rival voices
And outdances his seniors — takes his bride.

I have seen him everywhere, sometimes before glass doors
Going in with the last light of the day;
He is welcomed in his countless languages.
He harbours brigands in his eyes,
And trivializes his kingship with careless gestures.

An unleashed wolf with a human mask, he has
A hundred hearts in one body.
And so the king cannot be domesticated in his palace,
And the eagle's nest cannot hold him in a divine height.
And he rules from outside his kingdom,
The guardian gone out of the threshold.

MY SHARE
(for Anne)

I go far into every direction and come back alone —
I have taken every road to have the feel of otherness
And stopped short of burying myself alive in desires.

I take my onions raw, eyes closed.
Left alone with the share of a hundred,
I amassed their desires in one body;
And I am not more human than a lecturer.

I have heard the gospel that nobody perishes
From self-denial. I will be denying my self
If I should turn back from open arms —
It's crazy, taunting the goat with cassava leaves.

The dancer-god has proffered me his bounty,
A secret gift from his bosom;
Perhaps I needed only a thin haze, not a blanket.

And so I kick you when I am mad, regard you
In my sanity, and embrace you with songs.
If I am the Iroko, erect in the levelling storm,
You are the Earth that holds me rooted to your heart.

THE NEW WARRIORS

They had offers of titles and comfort, offers
of plots, offers of sinecure jobs, dazzling offers
so that they would laze about rather than go to war,
but they would not be lizards scaling the walls
of government offices, nor would they be dogs
yelping with party voices.

They had armed their blood against
the rabid bite of asinine representatives,
and they went to war to save themselves
from the astute claws of social brutes;
they suffered penury in battling against benevolent slavers,
but they harboured no shame in their discomfort.

They kept their plates in secure counters, bathed
with the same soap with the populace,
ate the same bread with the rest of the street.
But they kept their machetes in their wit,
fired at irreverence, and broke up treacheries;
the tenacity of their hearts made them the new warriors.

With their war they have moved the drought-stricken
to oases, shared in the agonies of the forgotten;
they have given their blood to anaemic neighbours
to survive untold crises.
They have deflated the colossal image of robbers in offices
and loosened the stifling grip of the wealthy demon on lives.

MY HEART
(for Obaro as he does a paper on the heart)

Desires flourish in the blood of my heart.

I have a desire to hurt the oppressor
whom I continuously stalk in my veins.
I breathe fire from my heart, not to burn any house
but to drive vermin from our midst.
I have the heart to scare the owl from sorcery
and outsmart the tortoise in its cheating game.
I have a desire to wipe out the people's plague
with my own blood.

My heart is a brute let loose.
It has pushed me from the pulpit to the floor;
and this has always been the joy of the heart,
seeing me down-to-earth.
I have cherished mean things because they are
my heart's desire.

I am hungry for what grows in the heart,
hungry to pluck ripe fruits from thorny trees,
hungry to see the Delta get a fair share,
very hungry to see Nigeria grow her own food.
My heart and I have a deal to stand by each other.

My heart is a conference room; only love
can give peace a chance.

LATITUDES

You can grow corn and plums in me
the same season; in the same soil
my hope and despair flourish.
The harvest has always been short
of projections, but scarcity has given me
an abundant experience.

I shuttle between north and south, pushing back
the frontiers of my skin. My chariot of hope
survives the fluctuations of extreme climates;
even in the sandy expanse of my dreams, winds
drive me towards an oasis.

There's flesh in the bone I crack, bone
in the flesh I bite.
When I am robbed of my furniture,
I am left with a new house of love;
when I fall down, my hope rises and gives me
a stature I cannot lose.

When I am a sheep, my lion heart remains in its den;
when I become a lion, my innocence goes on self-exile —
I have lived together with these two animals peacefully.
Hence behind every dark cloud in my horizon
I see rainbows.

THE STUDENT TAKES HIS LEAVE

The student takes his leave,
and the teacher arrives in the room.
I have never had the quiet I need.
Talk, talk, and talk is all they must.

They have taken me hostage ever since the chameleon
lost its teeth, and it doesn't seem
they will leave me until thunder breaks the earth.
One keeps guard when the other is loafing in his dream;
they are so alike I cannot tell when
they change guard. The teacher takes his leave,
and the student arrives with chalk in hand.

The day the student was arrested for making love in a church
with the chieftain's daughter, the teacher failed his class.
They left me staring at their photographs,
unable to solve the equation of their names.
The teacher was released, and next day
came to school to drop his course.

At night the student dances to bawdy songs;
then the teacher wears a sacred mask.
They fear that if we are all free, I will cuckold them;
but my bride is the one they abuse.

When the teacher threatens me with cane lashes,
the student chastises him for misbehaviour;
one hides my name from me, the other broadcasts it —
their rivalry has sometimes saved me from misery.
And who will blame me for being a tortoise in captivity?

War will break out between them,
and I cannot put out the blaze with my spittle;
these two are doomed to hurt themselves
or destroy me in their contest;
I am their only shield in the world.

The student takes his leave,
and the teacher arrives for his test.
I plot with one against the other,
but there will be no revolution until
I become their guard and teach them
to see themselves and me as one.

THE SENTENCE

I do not know when I'll complete my prison sentence —
I am deliberately kept in the dark about its term;
I have been moved from cell to cell, from prisonhouse
to prisonhouse, from town to town.
I am beyond pardon and there will be no parole for me.

I cannot recollect my initial offence; it surely sank
deep into my soul, a cosmic well. I did not murder,
I betrayed no one, nor did I rape a woman other than my wife.
I do not complain about my jail sentence;
I deserve it all somehow. Our judges are angels.

Friend, the day you were born you were sentenced to life.
For me it was with hard labour. The crib is Cell Number One.
When you talk, as talk you must, you are liable to prosecution.
I am cursed with a loose tongue;
I have only kept my secret with secretive women.

When I walk, I trespass sovereign fields.
I am not satisfied with myself — it is so lonely around
that you need some person by you to remain human.
I am still deep in the forest I had wandered into;
you get lost once you move. For each step I take,
the sands scream for breath; I hurt their nerves.
That is more than a misdemeanour.

I was sentenced before crimes swarmed my head —
how to burn a monastery, fix nuns up with men,
set the poor at the throats of self-seeking politicians.
The agents must have bugged my skin and eavesdropped
into my blood before I was born. I was sentenced
before I abused the hard-hearted President in my closet
and burnt a corrupt flag in the public square.

My crimes are sewn to my humanity.
I see unsightly things in hidden places, see
scarecrows donning dazzling robes.
No day passes without incriminating myself in my cell,
no hour I do not indulge myself at another's expense.
But before these I had been sentenced to life.

I am tired of being just a man, tired of being a teacher.
I want to be what I have not been: a guerrilla in South Africa,
a sailor in the ocean, a surgeon in a remote country.
I want to be shifted from this cell of humanity;
the air is stale with plots, false teeth, and bleached smiles.

I am guilty of complicity in life. I was sentenced before
I aided fugitives and denied the court a chance for vengeance.
If I do not offend the state, I offend my neighbour;
if I do not offend them, I offend myself —
my Granny told me, "if the world trusts you
and you accept the honour, you have to be its sacrifice."
That is the hard labour of this sentence.

THE MASK

My people knew me
for smiling suggestively.
They heard right
that when I showed
a pregnant woman
her direction
and she would reward me,
I asked for a bride.
(What is in a cock
skirting round a hen
besides showing desire?)
She had a male birth,
and gave me a friend.

Yet, with the patience
of an alligator,
I mined the mind
in a closed room
for a minute's blessing.
My longing fruited
and fell to me,
and I stunned kingmakers
with the ease
I picked right
my predecessor's skull
from the dynastic line.

And now at my accession
I leave my identity
to speculation.

WANTED: DISRESPECT

I call him names, but his face remains calm;
the tyrant neither flashes his anger nor thunders.
I know he is taller, but I will snatch
the falling mantle over his head.
His bearded praise-singers have driven out the diviners,
and nobody knows who will be monkey or gorilla in our duel.

The new crown, a nest with horns, still eludes the populace
halflost between the schoolhouse and the shrine.
Seniority still prowls the field,
and needed is the hunter who knows
how to knock down the brute with one shot.
I leave home to explore the wilds beneath the skin.

I need the sovereignty of Akpobrisi.
Who makes war with me sacrifices his genitals.
Reverence then to Odjugo who beheaded his master
to rid his clan of that perennial scourge,
and blessed be his lieutenant who stole honour from his dream.

I take my own praisename: *Odjelabo*;
the Invincible will get his wish.
I shed my father's name
that made me nobody in assemblies;
I will feed the old man snails, jostle him
out of the circle of men
and level his mound with his own spade.

He became king through disrespect;
I maul him to build my own state.
He says he is king, but he is naked;
I see no invisible clothes on him.
Bare, his swollen scrotum.
From henceforth our frontier will be a graveyard;
the land be its own guard.
My offspring after this pact will be warriors.

WHEN WE HAVE TO FLY

And if our tormentors walk, we have to run;
if they run, we have to fly with a tireless heart.
These tyrants palaced in fleshpots threaten
to incapacitate our hopes with blows, threaten
to ruin our peace with a nightmare of unending days.

There are drawers stacked with dreams in the head,
where a throng of artisans build monuments for life —
there's enough energy in our resolve
to drive us through rough terrains;
there are enough fountains in the heart
to keep us strong in the torture-house.

But imagine the poet separated from his retinue of words,
or a boatman compelled to make a bonfire of his paddles . . .
Since our tormentors try to bog our motor with sand,
we have to outstretch them with speed.

Because we are tender, we need a fortress
to secure our cherished beauty; we need silos
to protect a vulnerable visibility.
Because we are sweet, we will be consumed
if we do not ward off connoisseurs with brine.

And if our tormentors sit, we have to climb;
if they climb, we have to jump . . .

EXILE

When I contemplate exile
the tyrant who tramples my beautiful country
adds bilboes to my handcuffs;
I live in the dark hole of his hysteria.
His god relishes drinking the blood of agony.

When I contemplate exile
my land wears a monstrous mask —
the fruits lose their cherished taste,
fish desert the waters,
and the earth shudders under human steps.
I begin to see everybody as an agent,
and I care not if we are separated forever.

The atrocities perpetrated against Brutus
weigh heavily upon my tormented heart.
I want to leave my father and mother
for the cosmopolis of learning.
Solzhenitsyn beckons me out of this gulag,
Joyce wants me out of this philistine dirt;
I begin to sit with Milosz, entertain Cheney-Coker,
and play butterflies with Nabokov.

I have mapped out my escape routes,
rehearsed unfamiliar steps in a common outfit.
Surely a plastic surgeon has to mend my nose
and eliminate my scars
if I am to steal past the guards
who aim their rifles at the heart of the land
I want to flee.
The exile will only begin across the border.

Exile has become my seductress;
I daydream of her fine eyes, hallucinate
over her appeal . . .
But who will sing the savage song
to rid the beautiful land of the monstrous scourge?

GRANNY'S BLESSING

Granny said she buried my birthcord beside an iroko
on which an eagle nested;
but my hands peel in my father's smallest farm.
I served a decade to raise my bride's price,
and imagine how sullen I appeared to my people
when a cobra chased her from the chamber
before night swathed us, one body.

I am on the road with a pocket drum,
and I am never drunk except with songs, never bright
except when calling my favourite gods their praisenames
and annoying those who knock each other's teeth.

People call me lazybones to my hearing, saying
by the hour I reach my destination, stars will be my hosts.
No one has called me out to wrestle with him,
no one has struck me, or broken my bones,
and yet I am the weakling. I am poor
because I chew the dry end of an abandoned chewingstick.
They do not see me in the deserter's mask crossing fields
with a dog's breath at night.

Since the old woman died, I have been wondering
whether birds or trees are my best friends;
I could not shoot a sunbird in the cassava farm,
nor have I felled a fir tree all the years.
I move on, repeating what she intoned: "The iroko cannot
be hidden in the company of weeds,
and the eagle will soar to his perch
after feasting with sunbirds on the low brushes."

And it's not yet noon in God's day.

I WILL BE A BLUEJAY

I crawl through battlefronts,
Conjuring freedom from the stars.
I wear an apron of belief to cross open fields,
Pluck nerves from my guides, bulletproof.

The beasts of night vanish at dawn,
And I become my own guide
Belching out yesterday's drunkenness into a ditch.
I am a tortoise if I steal back
What is robbed from me.

My tattoos are abused as scars
Of a past life. Plastic surgery is recommended.
If the world is sane with grass, gaiety, and prejudice,
I will be a bluejay crowing in a tropical dome.

At my destination I will no longer live in a rock,
Neither move on guard nor sleep halfawake.
There, I will strut like a bull — free.

MOVEMENT

I fled a nightmare across frontiers,
Lived freely in a foreign land
Until the *Alien's Law* dispossessed me
And threw me on the road home.
After my rescue from misery
By family contributions,
I am pressed hard again.
When clouds darkened in the West,
Residents there abandoned their homes
For refuge under a clear sky;
The same storm struck them in the East.
My life has been movement
One way or another,
And sideways, frontward, or backward,
Who knows where safety lies?

*The Alien's Law during the Busia regime made many Nigerians resident in Ghana to leave for home.

A BOTTLE IN THE PIT

Soyinka threw a corked bottle in a pit;
It had no label.
Nobody knew what brew,
Dung, or hoax —
It defied telescopic eyes;
Pilots were blind before it,
Shouldn't a bottle, needed
As it might be,
Show its content in a general way?
No luminence will violate it
That is not lit
In a cult, subhumed.
Or else the sun whirls sand
Into peering eyes.
If the bottle is broken,
Who knows whether bees
Or even dragons
Breathe in that serenity?
There's no reflection
To tell.
It might be an empty bottle
Being mystified
For want of wine,
For want of water —
Since we moved our clan
And changed our dance steps,
Drought has been our concern,
A vagabond suggested
And he was clapped out of the hall;
But before he stepped over the threshold
Turned back, shouting
Leave Oyin's car in its wreck.
We took it to mean the bottle.
Whatever was in the bottle
Was brewed when Soyinka
Was alone with God

Sharing the same bed
With cockroaches, angels
Of Kirikiri.
The bottle in the pit
Was, after all, dark
Like ashes
No, like gunpowder
No, congealed blood.
It smells like a vampire's cache.
The vagabond had slipped in again.
The oracle only tells the truth
Cocooned in words, scanty
Enough for a sound —
No patience to talk straight,
Go the whole length of a familiar road
Before the spirit flags.
The bottle lies in the pit
Secure in its world.
Make a mound on it
And forget it.
It's a bottle;
Not all the ants, beetles, and rodents
Can eat away its smooth skin.
Break it.
Anarchist, shut your mouth.
There may be salvation yet
For us in that pit.
Let's place it on a hilltop
O mount a hilltop.
But the bottle will roll down
And find its way to its pit.
Foolish teacher, lockjaw
To your sore mouth.
Ifa, Ominigbo, Arochukwu,
Tell us the love in our lives
Tell us the death in our hearts.

Bring us revolutions to sweep
Our souls, clear our eyes
Open our closed roads
Strike our detractors.
Fly in experts with computers
Laden with data
From prehistory;
What precision will elude the researchers
Who know the number of sands
Drifting into the Atlantic?
They will recycle the bottle
With arguments
Into ideological positions.
Is a bottle in a pit
Not a weapon against attacks,
Offensive against a shallow idol?
Let's dance around the bottle in the pit,
Break our stilts in a final
Apocalyptic bid to see in the night.
But let no one
Spite divine gifts,
Let no one laugh
At the tears of prophets.

AFTER THE FLIGHT

The world gets bigger and fainter until it is nought.
After I ran a frightful speed, this iroko separates me
From a hyena waiting below to tear me up;
My heart's a mortar pounded by invisible hands.
If I could climb to the moon from this height,
Nothing would be after me forever.
But who knows
Whether the beast will steal there with its ghostface
And throng heaven with bad memories?
Many times I thought the end had come, but always
Only the hyena's shadow threatened me with bristles.
Osonobrughwe, save me from the fate of the careful child
Who did not return from his distant errand;
Lead me through the evil forest of life and bring me
Back home. And my soul, stand firm.

*Osonobrughwe is the Supreme God of the Urhobo people of the Delta area of Nigeria.

WHEN I AM ALONE

When I am alone
I go far to gather wood
And stray into an evil forest.
I cannot run fast with my pack.
Where the spirits catch me
Will be my path's end.
When I am alone
I move through streets
With everted lips and slit eyes,
A mask to induce a vision.
I bruise my back, wrestling
With marauders in dark places.
When I am alone
I light candles in my closet
And search for what I hid from myself.
I was born into some obscure cradle
And I finger my way into the vast sun.

LABYRINTHS OF THE DELTA

I.

We took off without thought of where we were going,
And paths opened for our anxious feet.
It was not for fun men and women split from bed,
Not for fun mothers ran with babies on their backs;
We rushed into the vast night
Living, not in our homes
But caravaned in hope.

"Where are we going?" children asked their parents.
"Where you will grow up, a place destined for us."

We had not known we were so many
Biting stone in suffocating shrines;
We took heart in the crowd —
We all had gone through disconsolate days.

Ogiso choked flaming faggots into men's throats,
Castrated the manly among us, and
Fell on anybody he loved or scorned.
We wept at night
Since we could not deny our blood in him;
We wept for the awfulness of our lives,
But could not wash the blood with tears.
We knew we had not come to our own home.

II.

Let us go to the River
With drums, goats, and cowries;
Let us go, draped in our favourite madras,
Powdered and perfumed;
Let us go to her.
She called us this way,
And we came, absorbing accents
Into our tongue.

O Water Bride
Moving without a boat in deep waters,
You heeded the anguished cries of our souls,
Ferried us fugitives across the midstream torrents;
You made us calabashes on the water
And delivered us on the bank, giving us
The virgin beauty of the Delta.
Who until now in a clear voice
Told us we had a place,
And we had been running in the dark
From the cat's eyes of our tormentors?
                                        We thank you,
But what words can fully tell the depth
Of our feeling? Your name on our lips,
Eternal glory to the Bride.

III.

You stood here, waiting since the beginning of time,
O Soil, to give yourself to us, and here we are.

When we came to the irokos, we saw ourselves in full light,
And grew taller by several fingers.
We tasted the first laughter of our adult lives,
And knew we had arrived at our God-built home.
At the River with a thousand branches we downed
What remained of a bare existence —
We brought along Aridon, our memory,
And Uhaghwa, our voice for songs.

Let daily rain beat our heads;
We have had so much drought
That we would sleep in rain.

The iguana ran to us like a god to his people;
We offered it eggs to remain our friend.
The *ogbodu* bird ran here and there on stilts —
So much grace in the party that welcomed us.

We did not fall from the sky, we did not
Pop out of holes. Our first home was northern,
And we had lived there from the time man set foot
On the earth. It was beyond the hot sands;
We crossed a thousand frontiers to be ourselves.
In our flight a god-usurping man tantalized us with security
In a walled town, and bound some of us for sacrifice
To dreamed-up gods.
A thousand frontiers we came through,
Each with its own torments.

Come and dance
It is here we dance
Come and dance
It is on this land we dance
Come and dance
It is on this soil we dance

IV.

Before God's praisenames were peddled about in a platter,
The Delta was one region:
A tropical garden where you picked for free
Whatever appealed to your constitution.
The land carried people on its back, proffering bounties.
The sea opened its mouth, a watchdog at the gate,
And into it Urhiapele found its way, glittering,
Paraded by mermaids, acolytes of love.
Streams ran through the landscape,
And the world stood on firm feet:
Irokos, mahoganies, the earth's props.
With the sun life was an invaluable gift
Wrapped in green foliage.

When God became everyone's flag and mask,
Conquistadors drove gunboats from the Atlantic,
Crossed the air, destroyed the foetuses spawning in wombs,
And opened up the land into whitelaced shrines.

They drove stakes into the labyrinths of the Delta, fearing
They would wander into cannibalistic snares.
Then flashing gold at our faces, broke our love,
And split the fold into liveried bands.

> Turn the tortoise back, O Waters,
> Bring him back
> Spare him mishap on the way
> Bring him back to me;
> He broke not only my hands
> But also my legs and ribs;
> Bring him back to me
> Spare him mishap on the way here
> And let the villain taste
> What he inflicted on me
> From my own hands.

V.
The River swells with boats, a regatta for statehood,
And throughout the land a warriors' dance at homecoming.
The task is done, and we mark the victory;
Our sweat is no more of hardship but mirrors of joy.

In the thronged assembly, gods and men:
Uhaghwa in a feather-hat singing of the love we owe the land;
Abadi, axe in hand; Egba with his leonine dog;
And in our midst numerous deities, some unheard of
But bearing our names. They have come back, the dead,
Moved by our thumping feet, voices, and drums:
For his dedication, Kwokori will be our main street;
May Essi's matchet no longer be raised against neighbours,
But against robbers of the new-found home;
Mowarin, my namesake, telling us great things are coming;
Okitiakpe, singing and dancing as no man has ever done;
And thousands — the couriers whose blood was libation abroad —
They have come to the concourse, happy spirits.

Uvo! Ogidigbo! Your names will endure like the sky.
After you were driven through half the world, you stood
Your ground and beat back your foes — *ama hirhe erherie*.
Not once did you go to battle without returning with spoils.
O you warriors, give us the resolve to fight for years on years
In the security of your shield of leaves.

Come and dance
It is here we dance
Come and dance
It is on this land we dance
Come and dance
It is on this soil we dance.

THE HUNTERS

When they were with us
We screamed, huddled into untold corners
Howled after their bite
Losing track of our dogged spirit.
They said they heard a wordless call
As if we seduced them into our bosoms.
They sized us up in their plans;
It was as they planned it:
Strike them and bind them;
As for their recalcitrants, rub them out.
They hadn't all the records straight.
We offered them poisons as homage to their princes,
And they perpetrated more ignoble acts.
We swallowed nostrum, placebos in closets.
If our guests told their minds, nobody
Would offer his hand;
They hid their wolfish desires
In brightly draped missions, testing us;
They got us bad, and became
More callous when they sensed we abhorred them.

The overbearing envoys have not always stayed with us;
There's some bastardy in their ways,
Forcing their company on us
Making us share their deviations.
They are already thousands,
And we are still discovering names,
Inventing them from our luxuries;
A few withdrew when we shouted
And put up a do-or-die fight;
Their frontmen trembled into the old trail home.

There's no taboo in the blood of our hunters.
O you who passed through the large loin
That gave me name,
Leave your neighbours;
Those are no foes
But fugitives like your children;
Wield yourselves into a single club
For the fields are swarmed, still swarmed.
There will be no taboo, no tears
In the blood of our hunters.

WE KNOW

We drive them
But they won't go

Open the windows
They are entering through the doors
The rats were bad
But we slept in our beds
The masqueraders are fat through diabolic cunning
Close the doors
They are coming through the windows
Before we close up one side
They pull down the other

Lechers are coming
Run away with your wife
Slavers are coming
Defend your birthright
Madness is loose
Take cover in a fortress

They passed the night, hiding
Emerged at dawn
Their human masks off
Scaring as they smile
They are swooping from the West
Slithering from the East
And anthropologists tell us
We advance westward
Mystics convince us
Love lives in the eastern mountains

We drive them
But they won't go
By the time they have penetrated us
From all sides
Our sweat will have gone down
Into the soil.

CHICHO

He proclaimed the East his guardian and factories
his fortress, opening a new road at dawn for Chile.
But the vision of national laughter enraged the profiteers
who had prospered in darkness. Innocence or dirt,
when hired Santiago dogs bit their own mother,
they debauched the saintly beauty.

Travel warily on a new road.
And the oracular truth came to pass:
the Black Eagle, bald from morbid greed for flesh,
mangles whoever refuses to surrender his wealth.
And so hirelings gutted La Moneda in a firestorm
because Chicho and the people had a common love for Chile.

This fall has benumbed feet seeking their own directions
since the Eagle continues to shower golden tidbits on rabid dogs,
fondling and driving them into untold meanness.
It suffices that the people still weep
and carry Chicho's name as their standard in daily dreams
long after their comrade is earthed.

AFRICA NOW

With alien sweetmeats trucked to our homes,
we barricade ourselves from outer gates
and bind our fate to unrooted pillars beneath swirling clouds.
If we frolic on the carcass of our totem,
a plague shall strike us.

    Hunters fired their hounds
    and took the bodies to our markets;
    turn down the plate
    before butchers serve us
    our brother's tripe.

For all the make-believe love and flair
for a surrogate identity, black brothers and sisters,
we stab ourselves with imported swords.
The chieftain, a resurrected tortoise, is the obese head
in a landscape of half-skeletons;
and the gods have not endeared themselves with worshippers
whose strength has diminished with prayers and drums.

Where there's been no hyena, a cobra thrives;
a ghost-face unearths bones from quiet corners —
there's always a nuisance in every yard to cause shame,
and from coast to coast dung-painted floors.
And we await the rainmakers to trigger a downpour
to wash off the stains that mar our common face.

    In a prevalent drought
    a splash uplifts the spirit;
    the raised head of a wanderer
    meets an odour of hope.

But if we wait for the outside world to approve a role for us
while others climb over our heads
and fly with dexterity,
we shall forever remain on the ground
and never raise ourselves . . .

INDIRECT SONG

It's only indirect songs
We must sing aloud
To escape the fiery eyes
Of power. Lest a mighty staff
Knock out our brains,
And the Chief toast peace with our skulls.

Those who led him to the throne
And those who stayed away
Have become his offerings —
Fresh and dry leaves
Consume together
In his blaze.

The elders lived with it,
Never abused Ogiso
To his face,
And died with the belief
That even the reign of the lion
Ends with age.

Only the exile trumpets
His savage convictions
And still sleeps
Without plainclothed officers
Breaking in
To castrate and blind him.

For now, the hornblasts
That can startle the lion
Vibrate within the free cave
Of the mind;
And I, sole occupant,
Enjoy this sweet savagery.

CONSCRIPTED SWEAT

Only the very day they are needed
are they remembered:
the storm breaks
and all lend their skills to keep things together;
the storm ends
and the commanders share the glory to themselves
without the invisible hands
that make the egoist
fatten his image and stomach
with conscripted sweat and blood —
a moat and walls to defend one man's empire,
a pyramid to perpetuate a dishonest name.
And the numberless shadows put flesh
into an inhuman ambition
limbs straining themselves to sacrifice
to save a diseased head
and only the very day they are used
are they remembered.

ANTITHESIS

You have changed religions thrice this year,
And now you're a cultist. You click skulls of champagne
To celebrate camaraderie with Nguema and Duvalier.
You say I have a nose that smells rot in a clean mind,
Eyes that transform everything into a scarecrow;
You say that my ears hear cries from a coffin.
And you make believe you're cultivating peace in a hungry land.
Beat your chest, for once you give orders there are boys
More than ready to put flesh into your shadow:
A fathomless moat and machine guns to ring your palace,
And a stone pyramid to perpetuate your name.

You clubbed one of my sons' head for refusing your livery,
Hanged another in the hot air for crying revolution,
And kicked yet another from the tower jail to the street concrete
For displaying the bruises you earlier inflicted on him.
My family has become an evergreen tree that has shed its leaves.
And now I am in a madhouse, dancing with whores
You hired to tease me into an erection.
At night I shall play cards, again losing to my dead sons . . .
You will blow me up for shaking you in your fortress,
And peace shall come. Peace shall appear in the lonely streets
On crutches or in a stretcher, taking wreaths to our graves.

MESSAGE OF LUST

I.
TIGERS OWN the homes,
Where shall the goats sleep;
Where shall the travelling virgins sleep
In a village of lust?

Grave problems drive sleep away.
It is dawn and the virgins
Are not deflowered;
The goats are alive.

When the vulture came to the market
There was no food;
The coffin-seller is unhappy
Because there is no sale.
How can we be safe without
Carrying our heads in a strong shell;
How can our fortunes reach home
Without encountering armed robbers?

II.
The fowl is guzzling corn,
It knows not how much it is bought;
The cook is frying eggs,
He feels not the bruise of the hen's anus;
Soldiers are firing bullets into the crowd,
They will boast of those they have killed;
The Pay and Records boys are riding Yamaha,
They are paying and wrecking Nigeria.
Sadat and Sadek are threatening,
The recruits will fight the Israelis.

Recruits fight the war,
The world congratulates
And remembers the generals.

III.
The giant marched through the cassava farm,
And they say no plant was touched;
They will also shoot the chameleon
And deny they are oppressors, deny their guilt.

When shall wars end?
Diplomats do not know; the bedbug
Does not care for the taste of your blood.

TO THE BULL

Let us smile
As you take us
To the stars;
The jackal pointed
At peace in the moon
And threw us into war.

We will follow
To the rainbow
But let us live;
The hyena tore us
Into bits.

Lead us to the horizon;
We do not want the deer
Who took us to the battle-front
And ran away
While we fell.

Let us eat and drink
As you conduct us
To the walls of the sun;
The tortoise sold us
To build his own shell.

Bull, let us live.

DEATH OF THE WARRIOR
(for Ramat)

The storm blew away the stars from the sky
And drowned us in our own tears

The giant who burrowed through hilly land to water
And knew the hidden chant
That would redeem us from a curse
Ran into a storm and fell in the street

The storm blew away our light
And drowned us in our own tears

He who blew pepper and smoke into the lion's face
And made the beast run into a trap
(We clapped our hands for a great one)
Was struck in early morning light

The storm blew away our pride
And drowned us in our own tears

The door that shielded us
Is torn off
And our home is exposed
To serpents and robbers

The storm blew away the stars from the sky
And drowned us in our own tears

The son who gave us direction
Is forever gone
He did not live to walk with a stick
But covered more than a lifetime's strides

The storm blew away the stars from the sky
And drowned us in our own tears

Consolers tell me
The warrior is gone
His lieutenant lives
The stump grows back to the same tree

The storm blew away the pride of the forest
And drowned us in our own tears

His inheritor
Will be pelted with taunts
If the promise is abandoned
To rot at the wayside

The storm blew away the stars from the sky
And drowned us in our own tears.

REVEALING THE SECRET

The line was drawn at the door.
The preacher shot hard at the elephants
Waddling in us,
Threatened hell for our elastic desires —
New ways of opening a secret,
A steel box
Stolen from the sky without its keys.
We are asked to rummage our minds
For pious outfits.
We pressed the door open,
And saw what the mouth could not articulate.
If a madman gives you a gun,
Take it from him.
And we did that for our lives;
We overcame our pressures
In a cold evening of communion.
But we shall not forget
Our fathers' names
As we eat bacon, caviar, and ham
At the preacher's.
Those before us were judiciously raised,
And we shall go back to them
Through the same door
Still elephants in our hearts.

AT THE UNITED NATIONS GALLERY

East and West
Growl at each other —
When one is human,
The other is a beast.
My mother is pawed about
By two masked savages.

TO A BLACK STUDENT

We've had no intercourse all the years, living together.
And yet outside you're a bitch.
You say the sound of disco music pulls off your clothes
And drives you into love. And here we are, a hundred years apart,
Singing different songs to each other.
I don't believe the tales about your outing,
But I will not peep into your bag lest I inhale
Illicit fumes. Your questioning was prejudice, and so be it.

I wonder why Barbara is so articulate and your lips lame;
How come Carmen so like an antelope and you dragging yourself,
Never arriving until freshness has vanished.
Your voice is a pitch too high, your smile wider by a grin
Your shoes higher by a nail, your blouse brighter by a shade
Your hair neither black nor white, and you're not a mulatto.
I am disabled by the thought of a ghost in a chameleon-coat.

Away from the other we are shameless.
You say for every hour in winter you need an orgasm,
And yet our fires are separate.
Do not say I made a facsimile of Cleopatra for Cindy
Because she is a rose, nor that I call you names —
She led a bull by the horns, whispering into his ears,
Halfnaked in her court. You hide your teeth from me
As if they are stolen items and not your own gifts.

When you were a bird on a rooftop,
I grew wings; but before they flapped,
You were already a serpent, shedding your age
In the dilapidated salons of Harlem.
If you turned yourself to a Mandinka princess,
I would build you a shrine more eyecatching
Than Hathor's at Dendera.
Three years have not been a long enough bridge
To bring us to each other. Poor Mama waiting for a baby!

I FLEW WITH THE KITE

I flew with the kite in a pelagic sky
Through routes located in my college maps
And swaggered that I had shut glass doors
Against a nightly succubus.

Pines, skyscrapers, and geraniums gripped me
Upon descent into the wonderland.

But ghosts broke through the transparent defences —
My hostess sleepwalked in our shared room
After infecting me with her strange disease;
I groaned, separating myself from her tangles.

I have traced the rainbow to its feet,
And lo, the rumoured diamonds are star-lit mists.

INTO YOUR HANDS

I built my home
In an orchard-grove
To pick ripe cherries
And share their taste
With favourite mouths.
I am not yet blessed
With round fruits,
And I send these halfripe things
Plucked by the wind
Through the double abyss
Of night and distance
Into your hands.

THE NAIL ON THE WALL

She did nothing sparingly. I didn't ask
What officer furnished her flat like a palace,
Nor why she decamped after a mine blew up Dede's leg.
Careening down a blazing tunnel, her passion
Gathered a wild pack. I didn't tell her
I had risen at noon beside a pythoness
And bathed in the same pool with a hippo.
We had scaled walls
And wrested a token from a bone-cast cloud;
A karmic hand flung us down
And we scampered, ants in a nightmare.
Then she became the lone *akpobrisi* to whom no lover can relate,
Raised barricades in the clearing that once held us,
Saying human beings are difficult to please
If you share one lamp.
Hence she circled herself in that coop, a copper gorgon.

Up till today she comes to me, throwing down her shield.
After her removal, goldrimmed blackandwhite,
She wears a silent mask whose red shafts scare me
On the lone nail on my wall.

BEHIND US

My window is grey with dust, but I know where
We first met in our senses. The old road swept
Through swamps and mangroves, widened
And plunged muddily into a lagoon
Where the islander beckoned me with a sea-smile.
I trailed her through the frenzy of her perfumes
Until low tide wrecked me on sand. When I cried
To be buoyed into her incandescent haven,
She came and showed me the luxury of her body —
Long hair, shaded eyes, and a golden skin.
We sang to each other as we had not sung before.
Today the lagoon is land, the road far behind us.

MY DAUGHTER'S KNOWLEDGE
(for Eloho)

The typewriter is mine, according to her,
And she is right. So are the sheets of paper
On which are printed words, hieroglyphics,
And the shortwave radio always by my ears.
I am the poorest in the house.
Mummy is a tycoon and owns the wardrobe, frigidaire,
Stereo, and more. Whenever we come back with things
From the market, it is Mummy that bought them —
I am the miserly father of a demanding brat;
I have only been kind at Mummy's prompting.
The big girl's brother has crayons, scissors, a tricycle,
And a room of his own. She has no room
And shares it with him. But her bed is hers,
For nobody else, except her dumb bear.
Balloons, *gummy*, donuts, whatever she sees on television,
And what I am too fatherly to own
Belong to her. And she is mostly right
About things belonging to their users, not buyers —
You own what you keep, each according to his grab.
The car is everybody's running chair.
When the balloon bursts, a penny's loss,
Or when the kite's tail is ripped,
She asks for another, and gets it for peace.
I tell her that whatever is mine is hers too,
But she rejects common ownership and holds to hers.
She has the *right* knowledge, growing up in America,
Where each person is blessed with his own.
I am the only commie left in the land.

—Syracuse, New York,
July 21, 1981.

FOR MY CHILD IN HOSPITAL

When the breath-wresting hyena stole to your bed
in its meanness, your angels were up,
and they drove it back by turning you into a scarecrow.
I thought my puppy had strayed into a diabolic rut,
deaf to my loud whistle. In another minute,
you would have shed your childhood
for an ancestral veil, beside Granny,
and left me a wretched soul in double agonies.

You would have gravely erred, for no rams
would empty their throats to fill your thirst,
and you would be a mendicant forever
since only those whose waists cropped a homeful
enjoy their final passage . . .

For once your teeth clench, not in jest of *Superman*,
but as you wear bilboes in your bones, crisis-ridden;
your tears mirror a gash too deep for your thin years.
If it could be shared, your mummy and I would relieve you;
for you deserve a playground,
not this grim shadow covering your sunlight.
You live on a haunted frontier,
and every day is grace enough to fashion an escape.

Decades ago my mother counted seven or more mounds
in the backyard before she slept, belly down.
By then the beast came in witches' masks,
owls with neighbours' voices;
she could not tell what bit, stung, or tore her young ones
despite her watchful eyes; she saw nothing.

When the hyena slipped back into our midst,
we threw our drums into kitchen-racks, cut the nightly dance
for vigil. This violation has brought us an anglo-indian shaman,
who is telling us about tomorrow: *Tomorrow you shall*

see more battles, but celebrate today's victories;
perhaps by tomorrow you shall be better armed . . .
Even as she talks, you call my name;
and now, the erstwhile threatening sky is all stars.
The drums invite us to new steps.

FIDELITY

Before Mummy came down the nine-month mountain,
I must have been
A thousand things without head, name, and voice.
I was the soothsayer's offspring of a tramp's love
For his host's daughter, born in exile.
Those that saw my greatgrandfather in me saw crab-teeth
And a mark in my right thumb — the fisherman
Had found his way back, canoeing into an old bank.
The mould was not cast in his likeness,
Because I was suffused in my grandmother's being,
Tattooed after her body's bird patterns.
Before I had a name, I was called
Anything that described my expanding likeness:
When I coughed, I was a goat; a puppy when I ran relentlessly
Or noisily enjoyed the bones of the oil-soup.
Before I spoke, words hid beneath my tongue;
After I caught them and brought them out, my voice became
A war drum in distress, a chant at celebrations.
When I felt like a white cockerel, I avoided clearings;
Later I grew an eagle's wings, and nobody knew my perch.
Before I had a simple longing, I implored the gods
To give me seniority before my elders;
I carried my head erect out of my god's shrine.
After I wrapped a crab with a plantain leaf
And it tore my palms, I discovered I was still uncircumcized.
After the pain, who would count on my fidelity?

BEST WISHES

He wished me dry-eyed, bull-faced, thick-skinned,
And would have me make others bite the bone they thrust at me.
Father and son, we live apart in bonded kinship.
He would scare with his bloodshot eyes,
But every warrior would try him to swell his boast.
Let me be intimidated by the giants, spires of steel;
Let me live as lazybones in the arms of tenderness.

O those gods speaking through the flesh with cowries and leaves,
They needed cash payment to clear their eyes.
They would have me shake no hands, take no kola,
Drink no bottled gin, sleep halfawake in my own home;
The theory is you never know from where the shot comes.
I did not throw seven cowries at every crossroads as demanded,
Nor did I sleep with a bedspread of leaves and barks.
Granny protested, but I went through the lone road at night.

My friends inhabit the cardinal points, and call me for carnivals.
"Will you be a tree, lame to the ground, when everybody
Moves the same way, heading for windfalls?"
Let Lagos and Benin smile at my back, let them sweat
In their hurrying feet, bankminded blankness.
What nourishes me starves them to death.

If I sat at every table, I would have no appetite
For my own dish, and I would be fighting opulence for life;
Opulence is an obese bigot, frying in the pan of flesh.
My articulate instinct is the most faithful guide,
Familiar with the bypasses in thronged places.
With it, no haste brings nearer my necessities;
No delay takes away mine from me —
I go round until it wishes me welcome.

No school will affix their signets to my soul;
No formula will bind my thoughts.
Nobody teaches me how to move, though many claim
They gave me feet. Let them claim
They gave me feet, also gave me desire to move;
I detest the sedentary life upon an office chair.
I will not forfeit the warnings of my guide
For a thousand certainties, computerized.

WORKING

In a tagged anonymity I go through
The palmwrecking, breathconsuming shuttles
That at week's end will settle my bills.
I dread the paraphernalia staring at me,
But I must work with them, the janitor.

Through the glasswindows of department stores
I see clearly where money goes.

I call the broom names, deface napkins,
Curse the sticky detergent. I am furious with windows,
Doors, and cabinets that drill me, and I bruise them.
As for who will sit on the chairs, they are dummies;
Let the seats burn their bottoms.

Through the glasswindows of department stores
I see clearly where money goes.

Halfway through, I rage against palms
That are soft like ripe bananas.
Let us be agitators, striking for human conditions;
Let us riot, burn the czars in our obese minds.
Let the sweat and sores of workers earn them sufficiency.

Through the glasswindows of department stores
I see clearly where money goes.

After the scumtanned formica, the winefaced urinals,
I snub clockhands, and bang the doors.
The dignity of such labour is east and west of my wreck —
How many will go through this tomorrow
If the raffle lands them in their heavens?

Through the glasswindows of department stores
I see clearly where money always goes.

VISIT TO AMERICAN INDIANS

Your body is pitted with awful scars.
I come to you, Onondagans,
Having, like you, been robbed and bruised by guests.
In your soil, Onondagans,
My soul mixes with the spirit of your totem
In the very bosom of the Earth
As we sing the same song.

MONTREAL

Across the St Lawrence, rising sundownward
Till settling on a hilltop,
Montreal basks in a cold sun.
Stilt-houses strain the eye's reach, brown.
Glued solid to his clan, the Quebecois
Teases neighbours with a native flag.
Circling the city in the Metro or walking down
Ste Catherine or St Denis, swept clean with French pride,
I hum myself a song, the wanderer with restless feet.

STRATEGIES OF BORNO

They arrive at night with snares
And trucks to loot her market;
They club her totem pet, spit at her feet,
And distill barrels in the bush
To wash phlegm down deviant throats
In night-opened shacks.

And as if they have been in a furnace,
They race out with cries of burning winds;
As if mendicants were their hosts,
They sing their children obscene songs;
As if they caravaned in the moon,
They speak eloquently of vacant streets.

How many know that the sun and blowing dust
Are strategies of the terrain
To stop raiders masquerading as lovers?
Her true lovers stay with her
On sheets of sand and windplucked leaves,
Inhaling her virginal scent.
Who imagined that under the cowdung
She vaulted her priceless gold?

And as if I am not in the same rut of life,
Living in the sun,
I wonder why she is not proud,
Surrendering nothing but mangled spoils.

*Borno is a state in the northeastern part of Nigeria.
It is hot and dusty many months of the year.

A VERDICT OF STONE

You fled this island in a bark,
breaking free from my embrace,
your soul shaped like a prow.
The island shrinks daily, the sea
closer by every step on land.

As I walk down the ruin of old blocks
into homes built on dead bones,
I know you were
Ayayughe of the tales,
gathering firewood after every storm;
pounding yam for the little ones.

No doors open where you weaned
a dozen mouths who swung you here and there;
no windows watch the cherry-tree
(its fruits have lost their savage taste).
There all is abandoned
except the soil God keeps for His testament.

And here I empty this bottle from my travels
over your head; the ocean deepened our love.
Since you broke faith with flesh,
rags sewn to dress you,
I discern dirt piling and piling up
at the beach, the line between us.

In your flitting twilight, you called
my name with your last breath,
and I held you; but you were already
irrevocably possessed for the endless journey.
Today I call your name, *Amreghe*,
with an elephant tusk;
the island vibrates with your music.

*Amreghe was my maternal grandmother who brought me up.

Part II: The Struggle to Be Free

For Angela:
in fulfillment of a promise

A camel is dear at a penny if you do not need a camel.
A single word is cheap at a thousand gold pieces, if
it is essential to you.

—Idries Shah, *Thinkers of the East.*

And there was a dark exultation
in sacred things torn apart,
and, bitter as wormwood, this passion
was a wild delight to my heart.

—Alexander Blok, "To the Muse."

GIVE ME LIGHT

The sun has no hearth in the East
denied the rest of the world —
it's not just who stays next-door to your shrine
that you bless with your gifts.
I traverse the earth with a feather-talisman
and sing you an endless song.

> Thousands of miles away
> a child bears his father's name;
> one blood binds them.
> One road, frontward
> how home-bound can the envoy be
> in this cosmopolis?

Uhaghwa, you are everywhere my god,
and in Yerwa as at home
give me light
that I may not live in darkness;
let me be the mirror of your kindness:
the wanderer in a boundless clearing of light.

WORDS

I seduce the entire tribe of words
that wake me with storms of desire;
they fill me with dream-seeds that fructify in my blood;
so evanescent, they flash their savagery in rainbows.
With their illumination I see the rut of the prize-game,
that wild enigma for which I have filed
my matchet, oiled my automatic rifle,
the elusive beast for which I apprenticed in diverse schools
to learn the smell of its name, the rhythm of its breath.
These words, blood-fledged, move me from solitary
contentment into the wide ground of discontent.

And today the black Ataturk will not sheathe
his imperial sword; no, the boatman who has slept
with the beauty of the river will not burn his paddles;
nor will I forsake my company of words —
among them are my bride, my first love,
loved ones, all islanders in the sea of misery.
For all the fluctuations of this destined love,
each day struggles to beget sunshine at night;
and despite their misery, my people sing
for tomorrow's possibility with a passionate voice.

These words have broken my prison door
and armed me with a fugitive's hope;
they side with me in the unending battle —
for the sake of founding a new generation of only lovers,
they expose themselves to fire, daily risks;
they are prepared to bleed and die.
Their survivors will be disfigured beyond recognition,
but they will have fed the new crop with their blood.
The boatman venerates the river-god, and the poet
seduces the entire tribe of words for his struggles.

CALLS

Here they content themselves with a sedentary profile,
hence they metamorphose into stones of flesh;
like subterranean roots, they do not move.
Not so the wind with its stream of songs . . .

Incessant calls pound on the poet's heart,
desperate calls snatch him from home
to storm the high walls that blank out vision;
calls to unseat the vanity in the national psyche,
calls to wipe off the scourge of his neighbours,
calls for a blood sacrifice to exorcise the demons
that stifle love by stuffing the heart with banknotes.

And he pants, struggles to complete the long, long race
for those that fell so early in the field;
he bears the corpse of the outcast for burial.
He goes afar with his songs to find the stranger
who will recover what has been stolen from the land;
he is the wind, his heart the sea that feeds it;
his voice creates a path for the warrior to move
his faith to the remote souls of the land.

So the poet waves the bright flag of his abused state
for the world to see the change — and what a shame!
He struggles to transform a wilderness into a city of light;
he glows with the blood of his bruised hands.

DEBATE ON NATION-BUILDING

I have stirred my tongue to no avail
in the unending colloquium on nation-building.
There must be some hour yet unborn
for unheard-of beliefs,
some hour to shock the world to attention;
many talkatives will then wake to thunder
losing heart as to what their voices can tell.

Those ideas not given a chance live as exiles
that will be recalled some day to tumultuous welcome;
they live untarnished beyond the ministries.
That suggestion knocked down by the crudity of selfish love
survives in the heart as a reminder of undying desire;
that solution kept away
as the problem exacts its inordinate toll
stands by for the hour of second knowledge.

I debate with rocks — phantom faces
I live with — to endear outcast hearts.
But there is the pain of the bruised tongue,
since the thoughts that can pour
a sea of fresh water from the sky,
debates that will open up cells
for a free march of desires
are all held back, savaged by ineptitude.
And when shall we all be professors and card-bearers,
when shall we be recreated into power groups
— the charlatans of the generation —
to be heeded for the worth of our words?

So I will talk to the trees,
discuss with the birds,
parley with human-faced brutes;
the dialogue for salvation has to be kept going
at the expense of traditional reasoning;
the search to bring back the cherished exile

has to be kept alive in dreams;
the dream to move a sand-bogged crop
to a fresh horizon
haunts me with its mirages.

The wanderer shakes his head at His Excellency's
insolvent mind, the fat head
who swung the electorate with sectarian frenzy.
Let it be, the land has enough to sustain itself
if only the blind back up the lame,
if the team will share the boat to rescue
imprisoned beauty from the boa's safe depths . . .
But where is the dog's bark registered on the game;
whose tears assuage the national thirst?
There is so much left to chance in our bearings.
The day we are turned right
from the nebulous path, then will we arrive
at our once-abandoned senses.

MOSQUITOES

These mosquitoes were here before man. So it seems
from their adamant posture;
they have resolved to harass and deal with us
as if we violate their birthrights in the land.
They have hardened their hearts against human agonies —
they take their cue from the power-wielders among us;
they have no constituencies to disregard.

From coast to coast, on trees, grass, and sand,
wherever there is water, air, and life,
the chorus of skeletal devils buzzes the ears.
Death, their patron, lurks in the veins, arming them
with invisible spears with which they bore our flesh;
at night they unleash their anger and greed
and replenish their sad souls with blood.
They are the witches that set families afire with grief.

They beat us in our own game —
they grow despite poisons, slip through the fences;
they steal, dance, overfeed, oppress, and kill.
But they need no offices for their wellbeing;
they know where they can transfuse themselves
and rejuvenate their organs with iron.

At first we belittled the race:
"What injury can this minuscule inflict on giants;
what fight can the airborne fugitive put up
on the oiled floor of the skin?"
Then we turned to insults — the emaciated cricket,
a caricature coat, and a starved ghost.
The insults did not wipe the enemy from our damned lives.

They belong to a bloody cult
whose other members canvass for casualties —
our doctors are themselves mosquitoes
sucking the people sick into their bottomless coffers
in private clinics, annexes of General Hospitals.
And with such godfathers, who will not tyrannize the helpless?

HARSH WORDS

Why does the look of my face confound soothsayers,
why is my head a balloon overflying a beer-dark sea,
why do my children contest seniority with me,
why does cold catch me in the desert sun,
why do I sing as investments crash around me?

The woman who will not sleep without me is my sweetheart;
I cherish the fruit that grows, ripens and falls in my garden;
I am spokesman in the company of the deaf, the one
who returns without magic tales from a glorious war,
the interpreter whose tongue is mobbed by harsh words.

Braced for the erratic fortunes that revolve
the atmosphere into a black-and-white dartboard,
I walk my pet desires into open fields
where time grudges me permanent favours.

I forge a matchet with the blazing beads of my sweat
to clear a path to take me to distant lands;
I pass through the brunt of being born
into a minority province, doubly handicapped.
But I venture out beyond the confines of the forest.

And I will arrive at the only reality that matters,
the song of my shortcomings:
my inability to keep my god's foremost commandments;
madrigals slipped into faithless hands;
a taster in the salt-market, his tongue insensate;
a slackening grip of the widening sense of commitment.
These, as the wanderer nurses his sore feet.

MY FACE

My face confounds soothsayers' eyes.
Will I be jailed for singing about betrayed votes;
will I crash on the road without meeting my bride;
will some witch subvert my star on sand?
They prowl my dreams for leopards, ghosts
and bone-chilling demons;
they end up disappointed by my reticence
which fumigates their occult horizons.

These experts cannot guess from my boyish looks
the iroko cross and tattered livery I was born with.
How can they tell my scandals which are buried
in the erect breasts of school girls;
how can they tell my crimes
from unpublished files vaulted in my heart;
how can they read the poem of my manhood
with the blurred spectacles of earlier generations?

They see plums in the cornfield of my heart,
they bring rifles and assegais to the harvest of love.
They step on each other's toes in their indian files,
trample the greenery with their elephantine feet.
They have crossed my forehead black
because they cannot see through me;
let them be blind to the cornucopia of songs.

My face discomposes soothsayers with its latitudes:
the woods inside swallow wanderers for ages --
how can a day suffice to tell my life's story? —
there are rocks in which the night buries its fears;
a perennial river serves my drought-stricken bones.
Will I be jailed for my loud songs;
will I crash on the road without impregnating my bride;
will some witch subvert my star on muddy earth?

EXCHANGING SONGS

I was bound to vomit somewhere along the road
the excesses of a monstrous belly —
I had thought that severing myself from a distant yoke
would be license enough to be *free*;
I had dismissed love from my heart
and in its place installed tyrannical desires.
I was bound to crash into some peril;
my feet, restless with youth, were bound
to overstep the path of sanity in their zeal.

O father, my songs to you have been full
of insults, self-insults on the mirror.
You have fathered a nation of tricksters
who are bent on dispossessing their parentage;
these renege on every honourable deal
to be rich at the expense of a good name.
And you have acquiesced to cleptocracy for so long.
If you still bind your youths to the market
and expect dollars for your human wares,
you will have enough from ready buyers!

Reach to the blood of your heart for a song for me,
sing your larynx sore of a new love;
sing for me no song of blind obedience,
but sing of self-respect;
do not sing of the virtues of wealth,
do not make of the new nation a roguish citizenry.
Transform me with the dedication of your voice
into the driving piston of the engine,
the filament of national light.

Let us not run each other down
in the rhetoric of the old egoists, wolves
that found themselves in the nationalist trail;
let us turn to each other a family face
and unseat the tyrants in our hearts —
we have our own blood to preserve
in the state house collapsing upon our heads.

WE ARE MANY

From birth I have been in the custody
of three overlords . . .
They extract oil from my wet soil,
prospect for iron in my bones,
and level my forests for timber.
Then they heap barrels on my back,
strap billets on my shoulders, and
tie hardwood to my sides.
"Earn a mountain from him
before pain or anger — some revelation —
drives the brute snoring in his face
to attack our throats,"
they counsel themselves.
They fear further change in me.

And they take turns to ride me:
one, two, three. One mounts me
as another descends — my bane
has always been the incubus of power;
the third busies himself
knocking out whoever is on top
to secure for himself
the comfort they find from my back.
They plot and assassinate
to benefit from my doom.
And when the loads arrive at their homes,
I am the shadow without its body . . .

I have donkey companions worldwide
kept alive by their tormentors
to slake their thirst for outcast sweat.
May this my groaning be a loud whistle
to summon our will
to shatter the burden and the jinx.

THE CROSS

And I am the one that must shed the blood
on which the big ones thrive;
they will only accept my blood type
which they say is light and sweet, so digestible.
They have grown so fat in the neck, so beastly
they know the forbidden dishes they consume.
They want my blood to keep the country one,
they want my blood to bring peace to the states,
they need my blood to double and redouble their wealth.

And I suffer the plight of singleness —
I bleed in my island, embargoed.
I bleed, singing my throat sore in the struggle;
I bleed from blows of the brutish majority.
Why must my blood be shed
because of my birthplace
for nepotic groups to celebrate their mediocrity?
O jewry of my soul, how many bills to freedom?

It is a mighty cross I lift
from generation to generation, from capital to capital;
I cannot count on an hour's good will, dressed
as the years are always in nebulous garments.
I have only this voice, an ivory trumpet
carved by the rugged hands of an outcast.
It is guerrilla war I must wage
small as I am
to live in this helpless land.

UGHELLI

To see her dry-skinned when her oil rejuvenates hags
to leave her in darkness when her fuel lights the universe
to starve her despite all her produce
to let her dehydrate before the wells bored into her heart
to have her naked despite her innate industry
to keep her without roads when her sweat tars the outside world
to make her homeless when her idle neighbours inhabit skyscrapers
to see her lonely when sterile ones use her offspring as servants
to regard the artisan as a non-person when drones celebrate with
her sweat,

for the palm's oil to be called the fig tree's
for the goddess of wealth not to be complimented for her gifts
but spat upon by raiders of her bosom
for one to earn so much and be denied all except life —
robbery wears a thousand masks in official bills —
and for her to be sucked anaemic by an army of leeches,

it is a big shame.

*Ughelli in the Delta area of Nigeria is an oil
and gas-producing centre.

WAITING

And the people, plagued by the hydra of misery,
rent the air with howls for deliverance.
They knew not the very face among them,
but they knew in their hearts' dreams of a saviour;
hence they would no longer abandon themselves in the hope
that foreign charities would minister to them in hard times.
They combed for the hidden patch of fecundity
in the vast barrenness.

And the suffering thronged the police for assistance,
but nobody attended to them for years
even as their condition deteriorated with desperation;
the police chiefs presided over crime and bribery —
they had not prosecuted any executive robber the past decade;
they collected private tolls in their caps on busy highways.
In their desks the bald constables pored over which
British or Australian teams would transform them
into estate owners, the last game of the season.

The priests and imams promised to commune with God,
but their sanctuaries turned out to be their bowels;
they contended with sectarian squabbles — death,
their heavensgate, was flung open by a current of blood.
The sermonizers were too earth-bound for the heavenly
vocation of deliverance; they loved their pockets and mistresses
more than their starved congregation and neighbours.
The people had no solace from the holy grounds,
and their redeemer once again became a Protean shadow.

Then the needy came to the university far from the slums.
The vice-chancellor's lodge was a palace, and
they feared the czar's dogs would bite them for trespassing.
They gazed at the stone towers in which
their sons professed their prejudices as philosophical truths,
but they found no self-respect, no veracity in the campus —
the lecturers broke their spines in skirmishes for promotion.

And so was no place where to go for communal relief
because of its extended drought;
the elites were quacks incapable of curing themselves.

And the army's mystique lured the throng
that knelt for every god whose banner promised salvation;
the generals were so neat in their uniforms,
so upright their bearings when acknowledging salutes
that they were taken for a rank of saviours
who would pull the poor out of the strangle-hold of misery.
But lo, the mutiny in the command post
left the officer corps perforated in the brain, left
half the people caught in the crossfire;
the dumb generals clamped down on the zealous majors.
The anguished ones might as well go to the jungle for salvation,
for the savagery there is without patent.

They had heard that youths resuscitate their fathers
from the sluice of damnation, lift them from dirt;
they had heard of youths bridging the gulf that divided their
    forefathers.
And what else with their heritage of proud customs?
But here is the home of reverse expectations —
the age-group that elsewhere binds the society as one
is here the knife that splits one people into tribes.
And so those who cried to the youths to save the dying
were stunned by the hardened hearts of the new generation.

There might be a democratic response to this plight,
since the ballot-box might contain manna
to feed the half-skeletons, since it might remove
the garbage from the national conscience.
And so the polls closed with promises.
Then came the legislators in smuggled cars
tearing at the state with wolfish animality;
the people were the losers.

And now, should they wait for one of the million robbers
to break ranks with the assembly and reform the vocation,
or wait for one witch, after wallowing in a blood-glut,
to break with coven and found a fraternity of angels?
Will one of the angry majors strike the root of the hierarchy
and release elephants from his sleeves;
or do the people have to visit the dead they loved
and wrest the arcane notes from graveyard teeth;
or seize for themselves the wealth of their land?

And they will find him, he whose parentage
will be disputed, a stranger in his birthplace;
he who will forsake his philistine father and mother,
deny their last request for a month's stay in the morgue;
he who will not throw notes at flamboyant mourners.
He will drive a beat-up car, wear the home-made;
he is the vagrant, the unknown wanderer on the road
with a powerhouse in his head, an infirmary in his heart.

He is one of the seekers, one of the parched souls
singing in the drought for rain . . .

MIRRORS

Now that the shepherd feeds his flock to brutes,
now that the guide loses his trail in his homeland,
now that the hunter fires at his own hounds for game,
now that the guard loots the treasury in his care,
the horizon mirrors perils.

Unity lost in house bickerings;
laughter once streaming
from the sahel to the swamps.
No heart can have its purity
in roguish cabals, shady caucuses;
the desolation tells in the vein.

And the regrouping begins in the shadows
behind a general's ghost,
solidifies before the party-torn alliance
of shepherd and his flock
the guide and his trail
the hunter and his hounds.

The ailing totem flutters to the low brushes,
abandoning its haunt in the sky;
it awaits the black powder, lead
stoked in feverish flames, a potent dose
the medicine-man in the shadows.
What thunder to rend the veil
for a resuscitated eagle!

I have only the ears of a singer,
a compass not in the department stores;
my eyes are the moon on the mountain
and I know the contours of my land, already
heavily eroded by painful sighs;
I have an irregular heartbeat
that murmurs a mad desire for change.

I SING OF LOVE

I am sick of seeing the land defiled by the priests,
sick of seeing such a great beauty debauched;
my outrage is rooted in the heart, a cry
to grow from within the populace a new life.
The imperfect growths of the years will go
and in their stead green robes, gold flanks.

Let nobody brand this land a given-up corpse;
I do not expend myself trying to cure a ghost.
Robbers, prostitutes, and drunkards infest here,
but the good Samaritans being born will fill the nation —
the elephant takes a long time to breed its kind.
Let whoever now sees the sky in its tropical sadness
not weep himself to death because of its moody face;
the sky will be full of stars, resplendent beauty.

Lest our inadequacies be read as a genetic law,
lest the generation's plight be taken for a curse,
lest the singer's agonized love slip into despair,
I sing with a full throat of my mother, my land.
I sing of the hidden spirit in our midst,
I sing of the redeemer in the womb of time,
I sing of the revolution incubating in the heart,
I sing of the pain before delivery.

A stone path opens in the wild country,
it footsteps the wanderer to his destination;
the land quakes in anticipation of giant leaps;
the cock crows, the night withers
the augurers, tied to doom, are drowned
in the vibrant rhythms of the lone voice
the day dawns with angelic light
and we wake from the nightmare of ages.

WE ARE NOT ALONE

We are not alone in the night fallen over the land,
but let us switch on the searchlights in ourselves
rather than throw about wads of naira
to guide us from the abyss in front of us.

We are not the only lovers who know the pleasure of sex,
but let us impregnate beautiful ideas, not
just fine bodies, gals, wives, or prostitutes;
we need to see ourselves in new blood.

We have all been brought to the wards of life
in cribs we soon fill with belongings;
let us not stifle ourselves with selfishness,
for we can only survive in airy rooms.

And in a world of adversaries, let us fight
misery and injustice in our midst, not
the seers who show us the mess hidden in our homes;
we need to be lifted out of the deep night.

ON RECEIVING A REJECTED MANUSCRIPT

The dancer dances
but without spectators —
a sermon without a congregation
to the walls of a cathedral;
stone-faced phantoms witness it.
The dancer still dances, wriggles.

And who is to blame for this farce
of artistic scaffolding;
who kept me in the company of stones
instead of a thronged square;
who dishonoured me as the towncrier of a ghost-town;
who taught me the language of non-existent people?

The dancer does not give up the steps
passed to him in his blood —
the mad desire that was born with me
but does not show in the face
seizes my heart in spasmodic forays;
and the dancer dances, wriggles himself
before his phantom audience.

Earth, be my audience;
lend your million ears to my chant;
turn your eternal eyes on the wanderer's dance
which a thousand roads have conditioned
into a new rhythmic vibrancy.
Let the forest sway with the wind of my voice,
let the stream ripple beneath my breath.
And then, what applause do I need from men?

I AM GOING TO BE RICH

I know I am going to be rich some day.
The wretch of a road will bring me to a new state,
where I am going to shed my rags for fine robes.
I know I am going to be rich.

I have borrowed from beggars and combed for leftovers;
wretchedness has taught me mean things.
But soon my misery will be published for consumption,
and I will become an instant star.

Then when I fart, it will be a poetic exercise;
if I shout, it will be cosmic outrage;
if I shut my mouth, I will be communing
with superbeings in celestial galaxies.

I know I am going to be rich.
I have never sought the wealth of cash;
I prefer it in kind.
I know I shall be sick of it.

ALMS FROM SEVERE GODS

The tribe's hearth has been too tame
to drive out the chill in the wanderer's heart;
the neighbourhood's love leaves him tortured
without the least knowledge of ecstasy;
the nearby well is too shallow to slake
his generation-long thirst.
The arena the clan provided, a bamboo park,
is too cramped for his audience;
the forest alone is not enough for his hunt,
who needs more than the same game
that fed his father's timid boast.
The gully-sized veins will not do
for his increasingly tempestuous blood.
And he struggles to breach the net around
and thrust himself into infinite fields
where he will crossbreed the seeds
that will flourish in any soil,
his desired alms from divinity.
O nativity, the birthright to contend with,
the slaver to overthrow or escape!

AND . . .
(for Angela)

1.
When I was leaving town, you said goodbye;
but that was a hoax, since
I travelled with you over the vast country.
You accompanied me into green cornfields
where you were the corn that teased my desire;
in my afforested mind you were the mahogany
with which I planned to erect a lifetime's home;
and when I stepped on the Delta, you became
the omnipresent palm, so deeply rooted.
You keep me company in my various dreams
and earth-wide wanderings;
I am the eternal wanderer
traversing unknown frontiers,
and you have become inseparable
from my expanding landscape.

2.
This day arrives patiently
in a simple dress of sunlight.
I have been indebted to this day,
slaving through nights to have it alight right
on this immense plateau of feeling.
I have consecrated my innermost shrine
to her who arrives with this dawn;
a handy mirror has prepared me for her entry
as I sing her a gift song.
On this day which arrives with a smile,
the heart is agog with preparation for a carnival;
the herdsman — I am one within —
goes with his own blood-sprung sheep
into the green fields opening outside his region,
his stick now a wand
for the glory of her who arrives
with this patient day of sunlight.

—August 11, 1982.

3.
On this new-found foothold, a plateau,
I take potent draughts from a hand,
an incandescent face, a vision of effulgence;
on this foothold in the heart
I sing of a second birth, fresh manhood.
In this thrifty existence, a beggared legacy,
I am possessed with a half-cup
from her high table.
From now this will be my saving grace,
for stepping out of here for a change
what a stifling atmosphere!
Today on this tender foothold
I am a bull charging with horns;
and what incandescence, what effulgence
my hostess on this high table
on her birthday.

—August 22, 1982.

SONG
(for A.)

From the heartland of my being I sing
this burning song that fills me with savagery.

This solo you hear from my ivory-trumpeted tongue
has been a struggle with girlish timidity,
a closet bride whose love
wreaks untold agony upon my nerves.
She offers renewal in storms
which dispose of my desolation;
though she slakes the thirst to clasp tenderness,
she possesses me with fresh appetites.

With her my song soars to an ecstatic pitch;
I emblazon her body with the story of my manhood,
and crash my lungs regaling her on trenchant songs.
And I empty this agony into another song
to flow through my bloodstream
into her suntanned sea of beauty . . .

PERILS

If you take the sting from the bee,
how will it still feed the world its honey?
Should I wear the cramping uniform of this age,
put on this ring or that, belong to some club,
and succeed like others through public approval,
what song can I sing other than of wealth
and obedience, what road will be open to me
other than the potholed surfaces leading to a crash?
How will I be fit without latitude
of movement, how will my open-
air cubs, those active lifesavers, survive
if I abandon them to dictators?
How can I sharpen my voice to that desirable pitch
to cover the antipodal distance between the starved
and fulfilled, the young and old
if I do not venture outside the communities
that throw titbits to silence me?
These forays deep into strange landscapes
with the tenuous mask of a loafer
fill my song with conglomerate feelings;
they make me more human than a lecturer.
And I suffer perils in these violations, necessary
to keep the head out of a sickening morass;
a journey through fire to discover a planet of love.
The process of alerting the neighbourhood has begun
in the blood with simple mutterings,
for if you take the sting from the bee,
you will starve the world of honey.
If I wear the cramping uniform of an institution,
how can I be my own spokesman, how
can I be heard beyond a closed door?

VIGIL

Today I need more than the roots of the iroko
to withstand the hammer blows in my heart;
I need the fortitude of the mountain
to bear the solitary incubus.
And I wear my cap low to harbour eyes
heavy with unending vigil —
I exhausted childish games in the mind's arena,
even climbed a ladder to the sky
(and there was no slip!)
but the sea was too much for me, and no fun.
My bones begin to break, not under iron
but under a slight mute weapon;
it also smothers the sunbird in my throat.
The tyrants, bent on setting me up against odds,
have got a rare chance to gloat
over my plight in this deserted island.
I am counselled to make do with look-alikes
lest I perish in helplessness,
but no exchange with whatever aroma
will fill this heart with its absent joy;
no mountain under water will raise me
to the plateau of feeling.
On the day which has not yet dawned,
I invoke my highland goddess
to overthrow the doubts that seize my mind
by bringing the long day of reciprocal tributes
on the heels of the brutalized heart —
words are not enough declarations
when two together can barely hear each other;
the needle needs the thread to bind yards
to swathe two in one . . .
I am pounding my head with the heavy
but mute blows of solitude.

THE SOLACE
(written to calm two intense moods)

I must grow fruits which when ripe with patience
will transform me into a sage who knows the wordless language
with which to go through the perilous labyrinths of desire.
Never short of longings, I set out from here
to arrive the same day with fruition —
who knows the decades it took to wrap the kernel
in all its carps; what schools the old man attends,
including those of tears at night and daily sweat,
to articulate in one breath his self-derived wealth?
Can I through a day's study exhume the burning
but buried hope that will be the joy of generations?

From this sentinel post, I look to the hour
when I will make up for these inadequacies,
for contending against the life sentence to a tyranny,
I need the solace of success to survive the hard times.
I don't know whether I have been overzealous
in already mortgaging myself at thirty
to see stars that do not rise at night
but the tapestry of my own making.

And so these desires rioting in my cranium
are testaments of my unfilled thirst.
It is waiting, schooling for the millennium
in the heart's grotto, getting there
with the attendant bruises of the rugged passage,
not being lifted there through patronage,
that enriches the savour of the produce.
This silent suffering saves me from charities
and makes the acolyte worthy of his goddess;
this double pain forges the vigour in my heart,
where I distill love from tears and sweat.

BEAUTIES

The world needs as much love as salvation,
the east and west of the human compass.
And whoever petitions — woos a goddess —
to rid the world of the miasma of hatred
propagates a gospel; he is enchanted by a beauty
into the wild park of solace, for
nobody with a stone heart answers the blood-call
to sacrifice his ego and invaluable gifts
to save himself and others from desolation.

And so in my love and prayer, I decry the law
that would deny people their true desires.
I am a lover-priest singing loud my faith,
ready to be hugged or hanged;
from this earth I rise with my songs —
spontaneous sighs, irrepressible declarations —
to consummate my love in a sky of altars
as I share with others
the very warm loaf of humanity.

BLOOD BANK

The casualty ward of life is cramped with
lovers stabbed in the heart
prophets lynched by their own people
citizens savagely robbed of their rights
leaders who tripped and crashed from their pinnacles
police gunned down by gangsters at their posts.
And these are not contractors bleeding from profit
not politicians suffering from cancerous tongues;
nor are they the victims of the rocket-assault on coven
or of the setting ablaze of the full assembly of rogues —
the world has a chance to purify itself
by leaving some to their fates.

The poets founded a union from the beginning
that attends to those brutalized by their egos,
attends to the widowers of deceased ideals,
and fugitives from self-derived tyranny;
they occult their sufferings in uneven lines.
For the sake of those bleeding profusely,
let them donate blood to the bank
each according to his guts
the blood refrigerated in their verses —
save the outcast from his taboos,
save the revolutionary with his firebrand,
save the freedom fighter with his blood-spattered flag,
save the true casualties with your own blood.

IN THE STRUGGLE TO BE FREE

In this struggle to be free from multiple tyranny,
let no drums be beaten
to alert the nervous world of my mission,
lest I be seized for sacrifice at midday
to ward off the scare;
let no praisename be chanted
to swell the small tormented head
lest the student forget himself and lose his scholarship;
let me not suffer the stiff sentence
I passed on others for misdemeanour;

for self-love defiles the sanctity
the acolyte holds for his goddess.
The drum when the robber has not been caught
in this vast afforested landscape
hides the tyrant, stalls the pursuit;
the carnival in the smouldering battle-front
sets me up for a fatal counterblast.

Better the task is done with the mask
of an adolescent loafer
so that nothing distracts,
and even the foe surrenders
in the shocked recognition of truth;
better I fight in the heart, fight alone
for this salvation
despite the thronged engagements
I have to attend as this or that.

And my love in humility,
my struggle in meekness.

ON THE ROAD

I have stopped for breath
at the dangerous zone of the road.
And before me the difficult terrain
that will disable the hopeless fugitive at first sight.

The mountain dissolves into a plain,
the abyss closes into a solid landscape,
and the twisted road stretches into a throughway
in the dream of the giant,
who despatches his company
to subdue the huge army of fear.

It is what I will myself
in the heart or in my unending dream
that matters before the encounter;
it is not waging unexpected battle that frightens me;
no, it is not delivering fear to the lion,
they are strangers to each other.

And so those windmills, armed demons at a distance,
lose their blades at close range;
the dangerous zone harbours no peril
for the fear-devouring heart;
the rugged terrain sharpens my fugitive desire
for the cover of distance;
the lion and fear are strangers to each other.

And so in my mind I walk the vast country,
go through the soul-searing ambush, unscathed;
then arrive back at home with quickened breath.

MOUNTING DESIRES

I cry to the couriers of night
to bequeath me their self-blanketed fluorescence —
every day a new legacy strikes us
from beyond the impossible recesses of fugitive hope.

I hawked my self-bred produce unsold
in the streets that consume *bonga* fish;
I returned with baskets of pepper and bags of salt
which they emptied for the day's meal —
I knocked down charity in a street fight
and returned home to an honourable dish.

I aimed at the Kilimanjaro
(the moon on the mountain, what effulgence!)
but took off with pullet wings
and landed with effort on an anthill.
But no matter, there are realities
farther from me than the moon or antipodes
immured in this crowded study of manhood.

And I continue to harbour the dream,
a bundle of firewood I have to carry
from the deep forest to my starved hearth;
it matters not if distance robs me
of much of the hope I bear in my head
and leaves me with only a morsel —

I aimed at the Kilimanjaro
without invoking the resident pantheon
of strength, thought and wisdom for easy flight
and landed instead on a remote anthill,
the abandoned outpost of the couriers.
I have been grudgingly blessed, for I have
added some height to a stunted growth.

THEME SONG

Collective output is the song
of the struggle, all hands in its banner.
There's only the sufficiency of humanity
proffered a vast world to cultivate for its needs —
what wanderer has been in the cordilleras,
a Catholic priest with Che's standard,
and still been an untouchable exhorting fellow outcasts
to breach the taboo net around them?

All the age-groups coalesce in this arena,
all ages merge into one needy generation
in a confluence of passions.
We will go to different directions
in the same mission for salvation;
we will all keep vigil before the common wealth
we will all share the pain and joy
of being born into this uneven world.
Our love will no longer be just a coupling match,
but a sharing among all of the sustaining loaf.

We do not need to march only in thousands
to pull down tyranny or trample our scourges;
there may not be a million bullets fired at the leopard
in one shot, but each stroke weakens the beast;
each termite wears down the oppressive prop.
Each rainfall deals drought a deathblow, copulates
with the earth for new growths.
And each wave hauls ashore its combed part
of the sea's hidden wealth; the cumulative find
builds a beach, a foothold of love.

THE PROBLEM OF FILLING AND REFILLING
(written after a trip to Bichi, Kano)

We always look for spaces to fill:
a school with pupils, a blank sheet with words
drenched with the sentiments of the heart;
life dependent upon longing and hope for fulfillment,
a register with names, a catalogue with titles,
humanity with births and deaths.

We fill time with a network of dreams,
silence with ruminations, inexhaustible habits
that bend over us to fix their schedules.
The world is a big zoo of masked animals:
priests, lovers, rulers, beasts of all species
their towns intersected with streets of savages.

And after the filling, we clear the places,
bulldozers and hands at our disposal:
make a road for our desires, clear the air to fly
for a full vision of our held-back paradise.
Then we leave those spaces to be refilled,
empty gas cylinders, stalls on a market-day.

This is the human fight against obstacles
told in a homely tale to fill a page —
the moon must be saturated with lovers' wishes,
the sun with the sweat and smell of their clothes.
I am the sufferer, half-smothered by desires;
I have filled an empty journey with meaning.

IT SOUNDS MORE CLEARLY

That day of salvation comes, it comes
draped in national colours;
it steps over shrines of dead gods, it comes
in the crescendo of possessing curses and prayers.

The laid-off, like stray rabid dogs,
threaten the city that bred them;
the hungry with steel fangs fight over the remnants
of the sumptuous tables of the rich;
the uninsured labourers at the chemical factory
baptise their sinecure managers with carcinogenic fumes . . .

The President arrives in a motorcade of Mercedes,
in those beasts that devour foreign exchange
and trample down home industries;
the timid people wear a mask of contentment
and welcome him with a dance that has no bearing
on their starvation, no bearing on joblessness,
no bearing on the gloom which swathes them
as night terror. Many gawp at the entourage
as a newly-acquired hippo from its zoo pond at tourists.

But the heralds of salvation are with us,
they mime their message in the street;
no one denies this terrible vision:
the earth translates the steps of these strangers
into a loud call — each year it sounds more clearly;
the dawn arrives misted in choral murmurs.
Every neighbour seeks refuge from his nightmare;
a common wish blossoms in every heart
as the sky flutters a bright banner at the horizon.

UPON THE PLATEAU

There's luminence upon the plateau —
that's the vision. Where else on the road of faith?
In the closet I see myself in multiple mirrors —
have I teeth of steel, a crab for jewels?
In austere days, a communion of offals;
our own screams scare us, shaken —
the great quake to drive us into the same refuge
murmurs in the bowels of our old selves;
it's a shame that the meeting will begin late,
at sundown, what we scheduled for midday.
With hope's wand I translate a tedious tone
into a wrestling drum — better to be delirious
than be dead alive; then there's still a road ahead.
There are signs in the body, bearings on the face;
so we have not come to a dead end.
But who knows what we'll come to with the next step?
If I see dust in the stars, cobwebs
in the galaxies of my right ear,
what have I been doing, janitor of the cosmos,
with the brooms stacked before my pupils?
What a fellowship, this umbilical game
when I no longer keep track of my dreams,
now a skyful of iron birds
tilting the world in a propitious direction!
This luminence upon the plateau, this un-
discovered city of laughter, pearls!

ANYTHING IS POSSIBLE
(on my obsessions)

I wait for the outcome of many things
which took off before my eyes:
an angel launched into space from my heart,
the conception of a new Nigerian —
I'm working myself up for a vision of a redeemer.
Anything is possible, either I see them
or end up singing into the night that will surely
swallow us in its cave.
In our time patience makes more demands;
hope visits us with a conjurer's tongue.
Meanwhile, I continue to wait, which is what I do
when I work or play; I wait
for the angel to soft-land in my heart,
for the redeemer to emerge from the wilderness —
either or both may come true, soon!
Do not tell me things had been cosier
than the misery cushioned in refinement,
nor tell me things are harsher now
than joy kept to die in a closed institution.
I'm waiting for the return of the cosmonaut,
I look forward to the rebirth of the Bull;
someone has to lift the cross of misery from here —
it is possible for everybody to be happy.
Anything is possible, hence I work myself up
waiting as I must in these demanding times
to witness the exultation of the double arrival
in my heart, my land . . .

RECOILING
(for Kemba)

This midmorning with a mountain's range,
I wave a wand that works only
at the precipice of a nightmare.
Blood spilt in the heart, tears
clot my mind, what a haemorrhage this desire
with the monocle of a Cyclops!

And time teaches wisdom over the years,
shocks us out of our shells with precipitate blows.
What gains in this harsh school
that draws out honey from the tongue,
milks the heart dry, and leaves us
with gall-bladder for victuals
and crushed stone for a cold dessert?

This school is a stern-faced desert,
and in it must we beg for draughts to survive;
here are we given enough space to wander
and exercise ourselves, grow;
here, only here, do we love without taboos.
But tantalised by adversities, we rub off
our smoothness on the dehydrated cactus
to be one with the rugged terrain . . .

After a hand across the chasm
of generations, a step across ethnic frontiers
precipitated a restive vigil,
after a pat on the back, steering right
broke down the edifice of a glorious image,
who'll then not recoil from strange visions?

Blood spilt in the heart, tears
clot my mind, what a haemorrhage this desire
with the monocle of a Cyclops!

I am shaken by the cold desert winds.
Nowhere does a man live shorn of desires,
but what shelter in this open, this turbulence
this midmorning with a mountain's range
with my wand that works only
at the precipice of a nightmare!

THE BITTER SMILE

She smiles with bone in her throat
she bleeds unattended to in her own clinic
— who knows who's on call today?
She collapses from the weight of her pain.

There are loud calls, there are frantic prayers
people scan the roads for the medicine-man,
the same roads that have been crashing their hopes;
they look back to a golden age buried in time,
they look forward to a millennium for survivors,
they look sideways and see their own shadows.
No one knows from here what plant will grow to fruition,
no one knows from here what is a mirage in the distance.

The bitch has eaten flesh to an impossible bone
and saliva begins to drip from her mouth;
Nigeria barks blood, she bites none
the loot turns to daggers in the robber's soul;
ruin visits whoever swallows mountainfuls of forbidden food
to prove the mad power of prosperity.

New guides are being recruited in half-light
to conduct people above their petty selves.
There is a big tree standing in the heart
there are stars above it
a thunderous storm will chase out the drought
and fill our gourds with water.

People look towards the arrival
there are many stars in the horizon
in every heart grows the curative herb
the maiden smiles in the throes of her labour
she smiles in the shadow of another age
the shadow drenched by regenerating hormones.

BENEATH THE SKIN

Beneath this skin my gods convene;
we frolic on the same, sometimes mean, things
before I follow them to their groves
where they are really their divine selves.
There I bathe in the water with which
victorious warriors washed their wounds
to tint my head with courage.

When the warrior-god I rely on
abandons me in the face of a necessary battle,
I take the blame; either I am starting a war
nobody with the veins of humanity can win
or I have not summoned him with all my faith —
at least, he needs to be roused by me,
and I cannot rouse my herd with one bang.
Who will fight my war for me successfully
other than the army I have raised and trained
to defend me with my own arms?
I have to be my own general, reinforced
by the exiles and outcasts in my own blood.

Power comes from the roots, from below
despite all the towers erected above us.
And beneath this skin, my gods convene.